Questions

-at the-

School Gate

Jodie Alexander-Frye

Illustrated by Rinny Frye

For every nervous parent, on their first day at school.

Thanks

I must always begin with my husband, Joff, who is my personal champion and encourager. If he'd have thought this book was a bad idea, I wouldn't have bothered - it's as simple as that. Thank you for your endless support and partnership. Thank you also for proof-reading for me! Also, thank you to my clever mother, Helen Frye, for her thorough proofing. A huge thanks to my kind author-friend Amy Sparkes for not only proofing but providing really insightful editing notes for this book! Thank you to Rinny for your delightful illustrations which helped this book come to life! Thank you to my children, Darcie, Noah and Saffy, for not once complaining that they had to wait while I asked yet another question for 'Mummy's book'!

Thank you Hannah, Michaela, Steph, Helen and Mr Peters for letting me ask you questions every day. I intentionally chose five people I didn't know very well so I was quite nervous to ask you, and pleasantly surprised when each of you agreed. Truly, thank you! I really hope you love this book…

Introduction

Before I became a parent, I heard wonderful stories of friendships formed at the school gates. I thought it sounded pretty straightforward. But I had no idea what a difficult process it would prove to be. I strode in, imagining forming bonds within weeks, but after a year of lots of waiting silently and the occasional chat about the weather, I gave up on the idea of making friends. I decided I was doomed to wait in awkwardness and should just focus on picking up and dropping off my children - why put pressure on myself to do otherwise?

However, as the years have gone by, I've been on a personal journey as a shy person, and I've made a choice to repeatedly step outside of my comfort zone. If in doubt, I'll make eye contact and smile. It's a great start. Then, on days when I'm feeling really brave, I'll start up a conversation, like, "Did you have a nice weekend?" Slowly, over time, my comfort zone has expanded, and I try to step out of it a little more whenever possible. Even so, the school gates can be a real challenge...

The interesting thing about the daily school run is that seeing the same faces every day breeds a false sense of familiarity, and yet so often our interactions stay completely superficial, even to the point of not knowing each other's names. (On the school run, my name is 'Darcie's Mum'.)

With only five minutes waiting together each day, it just isn't enough time to warm up and get beyond small talk. Then again, the sheer frequency of interactions feel as though they should slowly create 'water under the bridge'. Of course, they do, but it takes years, rather than in, say, an office, where the same level of friendship might have been developed in perhaps a month or so. We never do much that would naturally bond us in other situations or teams, such as eating together, or working together on a task. This is why conversation is often limited to the weather, the school and staff, the children and their achievements or struggles, and babies and pregnancies, as and when they come up.

I have found the school run to be unlike any other social setting. Of course you are there for a purpose, for your child to get to school. But it isn't really *for* you. You don't really have a role there and so it's potentially a little uncomfortable - particularly for a new family joining the school, or for the shy or introverted among us.

On top of this, many parents are slightly nervous around school settings, and cautious of teachers, treating them with the same reverence as they once did as children. When the teacher says, "Mrs Smith, could I have a quick word?", many parents look visibly mortified and I imagine they have visions of being 'told off' (despite the fact that the teacher is often the same age as them). I find it absolutely fascinating (and slightly amusing... is that unkind?).

So I've come up with an idea. I wonder if the answer to all of this is just to ask people questions more often. We only have five minutes, so why not be strategic and cut to the chase? When I meet someone I really like and want to be their friend, perhaps asking them a question each day would help things along?

I've decided to try it, and bring you along for the ride. I've chosen five people - three mums, one kid, and a teacher, and I'm going to ask them one question a day for six weeks. I wanted to interview a teacher as well as the mums because I've spent just as much time chatting to my son's teacher this year as I have to any of the mums. I'm including a child, too, because I also chat to loads of kids every day - they are always buzzing with information: how many house points they've been awarded; how they fell over at break time; their exciting weekend plans... The kids are the most gregarious and friendly humans on the playground. (If grown-ups were as cool as kids I wouldn't have needed to write this book.)

Incredibly, all five people that I asked have agreed to answer a question each and every day. It will be fascinating to see the differences between these five seemingly ordinary people. Even from the smallest sample of interviewees, I know I will discover some wonderful variation in points of view, life experience, sense of humour and interests. And I hope you will find that interesting, too!

So let's begin with a brief introduction to each of my five school gate interviewees...

Michaela

Michaela is a single mum of three on the school run. Two of her children are in the same classes as mine, so I see her twice most mornings. She is aged twenty seven, quite short in height, with blue, round eyes, and fair, straight hair which she always wears back in a loose ponytail. She has equally fair brows and lashes. She has a very sweet face - very youthful - she almost reminds me of a manga illustration. Michaela dresses casually, usually doesn't wear any make-up, and is always pushing a pushchair in front of her. She wears sport-style trainers, probably chosen for comfort as she does a lot of walking (to school, etc.) with the kids.

Michaela chats if someone else starts a conversation but otherwise stays quite quiet, keeping a close eye on her children. She is a really good mum. I really admire her strength and resilience. She puts everything into her children, and they all have a real sweetness about them. They are adorable, too - both her and her kids. She speaks with a northern accent, so I presume that she grew up somewhere north of Devon (which could be most places, really).

She is happy to chat when I start a conversation with her, and we are both Potterheads (fans of Harry Potter) so that's a fun thing to have in common. She has a good eye for detail - seeing potential problems before they occur, and she loves trying out new, interesting recipes. She's the opposite of lazy - whatever that is? Michaela has a small inner circle of loyal friends. I haven't known her long but we are definitely becoming friends, and I'm interested to get to know her more through these daily questions.

Hannah

Hannah is eight years old and waits near us each morning because her classroom is next to my son's. I am good friends with her mum but don't know Hannah very well, though we do chat about once a week and she is always friendly. She is average height for her age and has medium-fair skin with very dark, thick, straight hair, and puppy-dog eyes with long, thick lashes. She wears a bright pink winter coat over her navy blue uniform, with shiny mary-jane-style school shoes, and a large backpack neatly fitted over both shoulders.

Hannah is very smiley - she's at that adorable age where her teeth are a mix of baby teeth and adult ones. She presents herself as very together and polite. I know she loves scary movies, which seems strange to me (probably because I can't bear the thought of them!). She is very intelligent and confident for her age, and she has a sweet little brother who looks very like her, with the exception of the length of his hair, and the very mature poise beyond her years which Hannah possesses.

Mr Peters

Mr Peters is my son's teacher this year. He is average height and has dark, curly, thick hair, which is shorter at the sides. I'd say he's in his thirties. He usually wears a shirt with a fine-knit jumper over the top and always looks neat and tidy. On P.E. days he wears tracksuit bottoms with a t-shirt and suddenly I remember he's really about the same age as me. The rest of the time he feels like a proper 'grown-up'.

When you meet him, Mr Peters immediately comes across as very confident, relaxed and very much in his element. He is level-headed, calm and kind, and responds rather than reacts to situations. He is remarkably intelligent and knowledgeable (which he takes pride in), as well as being extremely articulate (I have been left baffled by some new, extraordinary words he's used on more than one occasion). His voice is low, his accent is pretty classic southern English, and he can readily increase its volume at a moment's notice in the way teachers seem to do. He bends down to chat to the kids at their level and is a very good listener. However, he does not readily give away his emotions or personal opinions, tending to keep himself to himself. When coupled with his confidence, this can make him seem a little aloof.

Mr Peters stands outside his classroom at home-time, so I often chat to him. We both moved abroad at the age of seven so that's a pretty cool thing we have in common. I have always really liked him; I feel like we'd make great friends if we weren't compelled to play parent-and-teacher. However, it can feel a bit like we're starting again each time we talk. I can't tell if that's down to him or me. One of my favourite things about him is that he's never in a hurry - he's happy to be right there in the moment with you. That's pretty rare nowadays.

Steph

Steph is a mum of four adorable children, and she is just as cute as them! She has such a sweet porcelain face with large, childlike, blue eyes. She doesn't wear much make-up (mascara at most) and has a natural confident beauty that usually only comes with age - however, at a guess, I'd say she is only in her early thirties. She's medium height for a woman, with fair hair that she normally pulls back into a low ponytail. She often wears thick-rimmed glasses, which really suit her.

Steph seems pretty oblivious to her own sweetness, and appears to potter through life at a sustainable, enjoyable pace! We have two children in the same year groups so I've 'known' her for years but never truly *known* her or any personal details about her life whatsoever (classic school run friendship). Steph is a proper old-fashioned mum in the most natural way: home-baking birthday cakes; coming into the school for kids' reading sessions and activities; arriving at pick-up time with a snack for her little ones; never in a hurry... all those lovely things.

Steph comes across as very shy and quite hard to get to know, although she is always kind and positive, and will speak to anyone who starts a conversation, never looking down on anyone. She dresses in high quality, practical yet stylish staple items, such as jeans and a striped top, or a heavy cotton dress, along with high-end leather shoes or boots. She has a Cath Kidston umbrella that remains immaculate after years of use.

Helen

Helen is the mum of a boy (Leo) in my son's class. Her son has Down's Syndrome, and so she collects him at a more convenient place in the school, near to the car park. Leo is very well-loved by his classmates and teachers alike, and Helen seems endlessly patient and kind with everyone. She is immediately warm and friendly, but, as she waits separately to the classroom, I never have cause to chat to her, so sadly don't know her even the teeniest bit.

Helen has auburn hair which is made up of slightly-frizzy, beautifully spiralling curls and always dresses casually in jeans and a jumper. She has hazel eyes and doesn't appear to wear much - if any - make-up (I'm only realising now that I've said that of all three mums!). Helen is usually standing by her car or perched on a bench and holding her car keys. I see her chatting to Mr Peters fairly regularly, and a few select parents who she gets on with. Once, I saw her boldly step out of her car and approach a grumpy elderly driver who was causing a big traffic jam outside the school. Helen did what no-one else was brave enough to do - she walked right over, motioned for the woman to wind down her window, and spoke to her. The woman was harsh and grumpy towards her but Helen remained thoroughly calm and compassionate. I was stunned. This is no ordinary woman. I can't wait to get to know her.

Helen and I didn't even know each other's names until I asked her to answer these questions. We'd only ever smiled and nodded at each other.

About me

And I suppose perhaps I should tell you a little about myself. My name is Jodie, I'm thirty one years old (I will turn thirty two during this 'social experiment'), I've been married for almost twelve years to my best friend in the world; his name is Joff. He and I have three children (who all look just like Joff): Darcie, Noah and Safferty.

I have very pale skin with blue-grey eyes, ruddy cheeks and thick, frizzy faded-brown hair, which is currently cut to a shoulder-length bob. My hair is the one thing that never looks in place. I kind of like keeping it scruffy and wild - I don't know why. The rest of me is always neat and tidy - I always wear eye make-up and I wear a dress almost every day. I think dresses are the most comfortable item of clothing and love the retro style of them and the fun fabrics they come in. I have a beautiful vintage-look (1950s) tweed-ish coat which I have worn every day on the school run for the past five years or so. It's wearing thin in several places and has been repaired multiple times (by my mum and me) but I can't see ever parting with it. I don't know why, but this statement coat, along with my double-barrelled surname, often leads people at school to thinking we are well-off. Anyone who knows me will be laughing out loud right now… in actual fact, our family is on the tightest budget we've ever been on. We make-do and mend, we invent, we are as creative as we can be, to sacrifice money and gain time, and pursue professions we are passionate about. We are so rich in so many ways - just not in the money way.

Speaking of professions, I'm a work-from-home mummy: I run the household; have the little one home with me in the afternoons; do the school run; and I'm also a songwriter; as well as being the Kids' Pastor at our church (which involves organising a team of volunteers, the curriculum, vision, etc., and teaching Sunday School). I'm also a singer and musician (pretty helpful for the songwriting), so I've become very confident at speaking in public and performing.

However, I feel so dreadfully shy when approaching and starting conversations with anyone I wouldn't call a 'friend', despite being notably gregarious within other settings. Only a few months ago was I able to pinpoint the cause of my shyness, and I was mortified by the cold truth: I care what people think of me. I care what these mums (and teachers) think of me and I want to make the right impression; I want to be their friend. But, ironically, the more shy I act, the more I distance myself. My heart's desire is to be a warm, friendly person (who I am on the inside, and with my true friends) and there are days when I feel I represent myself well - I feel comfortable and I smile, and I chat openly - and others, not. Other days I shrink into my shell, and I daydream, look up at the clouds, or read a book.

So this experience will be a challenge for me (I even felt nervous asking these people to take part) - but I will do it for you, dear reader, for your enjoyment and amusement! I will be forcing myself to chat to people every day - some questions will be easy to ask, others not so much. Now, without further ado, and with much anticipation, let us begin!

Week 1

Monday:

What did you have for breakfast?

Hannah: Nutella on toast.

Michaela : Nothing yet - I'll have an apple and an orange when I get home!
(She laughs about how hectic it is before school - she's too busy sorting the kids out. Once she's done the school drop-off she goes home and has a drink and breakfast.)

Steph: *(I don't see Steph on Mondays.)*

Helen: Nothing - for breakfast or lunch!
(She says she's busy helping Leo get ready in the mornings and often forgets to eat until the afternoon. She says she'd like to try getting into porridge. We have a nice first chat.)

Mr Peters: Half a small glass of freshly-squeezed orange juice.
(I ask if he squeezes it himself, he says no, and we half-joke about the sugar levels and potential for a sugar crash later in the day, which he admits to having. I say I don't have breakfast either, just coffee. He mentions that he doesn't like hot drinks. Then he tells me that when he was a little boy in India there were weevils in the muesli on several occasions, which has put him off porridge ever since!)

Tuesday:

What's your favourite thing about school / being a mum / teaching?

Hannah: Learning.

(She thinks for a moment.)

My favourite is art…and geography.

Michaela: The cuddles.

(She smiles. She tells me her youngest had a tantrum in Tesco today so no favourite things today, but overall, she loves the cuddles.)

Steph: Oh, that's a hard one.

(Pauses to think.)

There are so many to choose.

(Thinks some more.)

I love all of it. Every single thing.

(I remark on what a lovely answer that is and we agree how special it is to be a mum.)

Helen: I know this will sound weird, but when Leo is ill and we snuggle up together in bed.

(She describes how Leo is quite a cuddly boy but how extra special their mother-son cuddles are, and talks about that bond. Helen says how much she's enjoying chatting to me, "… even without the questions!")

Mr Peters: The 'dawning moment of realisation'.

(He explains that this is a phrase he first discovered in a Calvin and Hobbes comic.)

When a child looks at you and goes, "aah!"

(As in, when 'the penny drops' and they 'get it'. We chat a bit and he hurries off to a meeting.)

Wednesday:

What's your favourite film?

Mr Peters: The Fifth Element.
(He says he likes how clever the script is - the way each scene's dialogue flows into the next scene's, despite being at different ends of the galaxy and different characters talking about different things. He gives an example with a little impression of Gary Oldman. I say I only saw the film for the first time recently and didn't notice that.)

Hannah: Um...
(She 'ums and ahs' for a while, and can't settle on one. I suggest her choosing three.)
...Star Wars...Lord of the Rings...and... Labyrinth.

Michaela: *(I didn't see Michaela to talk to today.)*

Steph: Oooh, that's a hard one.
(Thinks)
What films do I watch over and over again?
Serenity? But I like a lot of romantic comedies too.
(I say I've seen the 'Firefly' series but haven't seen 'Serenity' yet but keep meaning to. We talk about the classic 1990s rom-coms we both like - our favourites include 'Sleepless in Seattle' and 'While You Were Sleeping'.)

Helen: I'd have to say 'You've Got Mail', but there are loads of chick flicks I like, like 'Sleepless in Seattle' and 'While You were Sleeping'.
(We gush over the films together, and Helen refers back to yesterday's question which she says she's been thinking about, and she asks me if I feel that same special bond with my children. I say I do. It's another lovely little chat.)

Thursday:

Do you have any brothers or sisters?

Hannah: one brother, his name is Aiden.
(We establish that he's younger than her. I ask if she likes being a big sister, she grins, "Yes." I ask Aiden - who is standing next to Hannah - if he likes having a big sister, and he smiles, "Yes, but she jumps out at me and scares me all the time." They giggle.)

Michaela: Full siblings or half-siblings?
(I say both.)
I have two full siblings and four half-siblings.
(She tells me she has a full brother and sister who are thirteen years older than her, but grew up with the two half-brothers and two half-sisters, as a five. Her full sister lives nearby and her brother lives in Bradford. Michaela's little boy is poorly today so we also talk about that for a minute.)

Steph: I have one sister, and she's younger.
(I ask if she lives nearby; Steph answers, "Yes," and says she sees her every day. I ask if she likes being a big sister, she says she used to get the, "You should know better!" line when they were younger, and tries not to repeat the same phrase to her oldest child.)

Helen: It's kind of complicated. I have one big brother and a half-brother a few years younger than me, so I usually just say I have two brothers.
(She goes on to explain that she also has lots of half-siblings… "Very expensive at Christmas!")

Mr Peters: I have one sister - her name is Meg. She works for the Galapagos Trust.

(I ask what that is and he seems surprised that I don't know but tells me about it. I ask if his sister is older or younger; he says she's younger and as he went to boarding school at the age of thirteen he didn't have a strong bond with her, but they get on now they're grown up. I suggest that might be one of the down-sides to boarding school; he says, "One of many.")

Friday:

What's your favourite way to spend the weekend?

Mr Peters: I like going up to Dartmoor and I like going to Fingle Bridge - it's near Castle Drogo.
(He describes the location and the beauty of it. It sounds lovely.)
I go there about once every three weekends. Not camping or anything though, I'm not very into camping...
(He smiles. I say I think there's something wrong with people who like camping and we laugh.)

Hannah: I like doing arts and crafts.
(I ask what kind of arts and crafts she likes doing - she says sketching and painting are her favourites.)

Michaela: *(I didn't see Michaela today.)*

Steph: *(I didn't catch Steph today.)*

Helen: We usually go out for brunch, and then go for a walk, and then go trampolining or to 'Bare Feet' in Exeter.
(She explains that they try to keep weekends as chilled out as possible because Leo works so hard in the week and gets tired out. I'm running a bit late so we say, "Have a nice weekend," and I have to dash over to collect my kids.)

Notes at the Weekend

Okay, I don't know if it came across in what you just read, but this week was pretty incredible for me! As someone who will usually opt to stay quiet over starting a conversation, I've discovered the power of questions. I feel as though I've been handed a key - to unlock conversation, to interact with others, to start to get to know people…

On Thursday something happened instinctively and completely unintentionally. I was waiting at the start of the school day with a mum I never speak to and who never speaks to me. We mentioned the temperature and she casually mumbled something about the temperature of her office. Before I realised it, a question flew from my lips… "Where do you work?" She answered. And another, more meaningful question escaped, "Do you enjoy your job?" She happily answered and we chatted a bit. This may sound normal to you, but for a wimp like me, it was a total breakthrough to be asking questions so naturally and comfortably! I can't believe all it took were three days for me to get into the groove! I'm loving this question thing!

I've also found it so interesting how the five people answer so differently. Some - like Hannah - just cut straight to the point. Short, clear answers. (I wonder if she'll continue to answer like that over the coming weeks, or get a bit more relaxed.) Steph is fairly short and sweet with her answers too, but does seem relaxed and friendly. She might just be a classic introvert. Michaela is quite chatty and friendly, and I feel like we're getting to be pals.

As for Mr Peters, I feel as though someone is slipping him the questions 24 hours in advance (even though it's impossible because I choose them the night before)… he pauses for but a fraction of a second before giving some incredible, well-crafted reply. I've tried each day to pry a little further to find a more emotional response from him, but I think it will take some time for him to be comfortable doing so.

Helen, on the other hand, has met me on a different level. By Day 3 she started the conversation by saying she'd been thinking about the previous question and wanted to know my answer. This was amazing - it means she was not only interested in sharing something of herself (by talking about herself, as it turns out most people enjoy doing), but she had naturally taken the next step of wanting to know about me.

I did discover some of us had things in common: Hannah and I are both big sisters to a brother and love it; Mr Peters, Helen and I don't eat breakfast; Steph, Helen and I all love the same 1990s chick flicks; Steph and I both like Firefly (I never would have guessed that!); Helen and I like a relaxed weekend; and I adore being in nature but not camping, like Mr P.

My observations are that Mr Peters and Hannah both take their questions seriously and want to give impressive and thoughtful answers. Steph, Michaela and Helen answer very differently - it feels much more like a chat.

I have noticed that I feel a bit less awkward chatting with Mr Peters, and very kindly he's made it easier by approaching me and asking, "Have you got a question for me?" I think he seems to quite enjoy it - like a quiz or something. I know Helen is enjoying it, because she's told me a few times and has also contacted me outside of school (on private messages on social media) where we shared music, a common interest. I will be seeing Michaela on Sunday as she has invited me to her son's infant baptism - pretty special!

Overall, I have been very pleasantly surprised by how Week 1 has gone. I feel a lot more confident socially even from five days of putting myself out there. I can't wait for next week!

Week 2

Monday:

Have you ever broken a bone?

Mr Peters: No... but I did have thirteen stitches in my leg when I was nine in India.
(He tells the story of how he badly gashed his leg on a day trip in the hills, and how he and his parents had to try to find a private doctor. I remark on how interesting even his not-having-broken-a-bone story is - he points out that answering 'no' wouldn't be very interesting for a book! I say, "Yes, but I've never broken a bone and have no interesting story to go along with that!" We laugh.)

Michaela: *(Michaela isn't at school today because her little boy is poorly.)*

Steph: *(I don't see Steph on Mondays.)*

Hannah: No.
(I ask Hannah's mum and dad and neither of them have broken a bone either. They ask me and I say no too! We all laugh.)

Helen: No!
(She rushes over to the tree by her car and grabs it - "Touch wood!" We laugh. She says she climbed a lot of trees when she was a kid but is too smart to break a bone! "Yes, that's why no-one I've asked has broken a bone," I say, "You're all too intelligent!" We laugh. We also talk briefly about our weekends and the unseasonable snow that's forecast this week.)

Tuesday:

What was your favourite subject at school?

Hannah: Art and Geography.

(I ask what Hannah likes about geography, and she tells me she loves learning about all the different countries. I ask where she'd like to visit, and she says she'd love to visit Egypt and see the pyramids. She tells me she has a globe at home and a picture of all the flags of the world. She comes alive chatting about the world and we start to discuss the exciting possibilities of alternate dimensions! Hannah says, "Maybe there's a purple rabbit right there and we just can't see it!" We giggle and suggest more things that could be around!)

Mr Peters: Earth and Science Studies in Grade 7 with Mr Anderson. We got to do things like work out the size of the Earth by working out its angle from the Sun, and cut into rock and see inside.

(I say that sounds pretty cool, and the measuring bit seems like physics to me, and he has a look that says 'not really' but he chooses not to correct me, I presume because of time. I'm confused about him calling it 'Grade' 7 and say I didn't realise he went to America, but he didn't; it's because he was in international school in India. He's told me this before but I'm not really joining up the dots today. Between us we aren't sure what age Grade 7 is because it was a bit complicated and he was moved up a year for a time. He has to teach his class now so he says, "Bye.")

Steph: Maths.

(This is the first answer like this that I've had from Steph - instant and certain. We talk a bit about maths and then the cold

weather, and I make a reference to living in Canada as a child. She asks what age I was and what made my family move there, and we have a real conversation. Then the nursery doors open and we all rush inside to get warm and settle our little ones in for the morning.)

Michaela: *(Michaela isn't at school today because her little boy is poorly.)*

Helen: English. Yep, I always liked English.
(She tells me that she had a great teacher at primary school and used to love illustrating the decorative borders. We talk about what an impact teachers can have, for better or worse. We talk about the snow as we've had some flurries today but much more is forecast. Helen says she's tempted to drive up to Exmoor after school to take some pictures of the snow, as it's settled on Exmoor.)

Wednesday:

What's your favourite unhealthy snack?

Hannah: Chocolate.
(I ask which type she likes best, and she thinks for a moment.)
Lindt. or Guylian. I can't decide which I like best.
(I say they are quite grown-up chocolates. She agrees.)

Mr Peters: *(He thinks for a minute. I add, "…other than the daily shot of orange juice…" He smiles.)*
Probably… flapjack? And I'm a bit of a sucker for pastry.

Michaela: My favourite snack…
(She's smiling and thinking for a while. Another mum starts making suggestions. I ask Michaela if she's more sweet or savoury and she says a bit of both. I ask, "If I handed you a £1 coin in a corner shop, what would you buy?")
Maltesers. I love Maltesers. But I have to hide them in the house.
(We talk about eating the kids' Easter eggs before Easter and have a funny chat about that.)

Steph: Oooh.
(Thinks. "Not enough to choose from or too many?" I ask. "Too many," she replies.)
I think I'd have to say crisps.
(I ask what flavour.)
Oh no, I can't choose a flavour! Any! I like them all!

Helen: *(Thinks for a minute.)*

Oh, I know what it is. If Roger and I really fancy a treat, we have a Marks and Spencer Belgian chocolate eclair.

(She tells me how delicious they are and how Roger loves crisps, but the eclairs are something they both enjoy as a treat. I say I must try one. I comment that today is the first time I've seen Helen wear a coat and she says its because she's been up on Exmoor taking photos of the snow.)

Thursday:

School closed due to SNOW!

Friday:

School closed due to SNOW!

Notes at the Weekend

At the end of the school day on Wednesday the school was still on the fence about whether to close, and there was a wonderful sense of anticipation in the air. And would you believe that we had not one but TWO snow days when the schools in the area all closed on Thursday and Friday, the 1st and 2nd of March! Truly bizarre! This meant that we all had an unexpected four-day weekend!

I'll have to ask my five interviewees what they got up to… I baked cupcakes, oat cookies and bread pudding; I had snowball fights; shovelled a lot of snow; attempted to build a full-on huge igloo; and went for a late night snow walk with Darcie, my older daughter. Such fun! We also drank a *lot* of hot chocolate and I got the kids to do a bit of home-learning to keep their brains ticking along.

This week was still interesting, though, despite being cut short. Steph asked me about my time in Canada which was lovely - I feel like we really started to become buddies this week. We chatted a lot outside of the official questions and it felt really natural.

Hannah came to life this week when talking about geography and suddenly turned into a total chatterbox! I think when you find someone's passion you suddenly see this amazingly authentic part of them. It's wonderful. I've yet to really stumble on that with the others, probably due to the sort of questions I've asked so far. And, in all fairness, they could say the same about me. I'm extremely passionate about a number of subjects but it's hard to go on about them when all you were asked was, "How was your weekend?"

I didn't see Michaela much but I had been to her son's baptism at the weekend and back to her house. I think there's something special about being welcomed into someone's home. Michaela and I had a good giggle on Wednesday morning before school - I felt my guard come right down as I entertained her and two other mum-friends with funny stories, just as I would at a party amongst friends.

I really like Helen. I can't believe that if it wasn't for this book, we may never have got chatting. Thank goodness for the book. She's great! So level-headed and warm and fun!

Speaking of level-headed, let's talk about Mr Peters. This Monday he knew he wouldn't be teaching in the morning and would be doing some training in the afternoon, so when I was dropping off my son in the morning, he came outside to find me just to answer my question. I really appreciated it, and it made me realise how seriously he was taking my book - I found it really, very sweet. It's been fun hearing his stories and getting to know him better. I hope as a reader you're enjoying the mix of people I've selected.

I have definitely felt my social confidence building up this week. There's a mum who was new to the school in

September and we've been getting on really well, having a laugh and chatting several times a week. But can you guess the classic awkward problem? We never introduced ourselves and so neither of us knew each other's names! (This is way more common at the school gates than you might expect.) Anyway, I was standing next to her on Monday and we smiled at each other and I thought, *just do it!* So I stepped up and said, "You know, I don't think I ever told you my name. I'm Jodie!" She was so delighted, told me her name, and thanked me for breaking the ice and having the awkward conversation! Since then we've used each others names with a giggle and really feel more like actual friends and less like acquaintances.

I loved this week. Genuinely, I really look forward to Monday and hope the snow has melted a bit so school can open up again. Four days of being totally snowed in is enough for anyone, I've discovered!

Week 3

Monday:

What did you get up to on the snow days?

Michaela: *(No sign of Michaela today.)*

Steph: *(I don't see Steph on Mondays.)*

Helen: *(Leo is ill today so no Helen, either!)*

Hannah: I built a snowman, and we went tobogganing and had snowball fights!
(We chat about the snow a little and I tell her and her mum about my disastrous attempt at building an igloo. It's the end of the school day, all three of my children are talking 'at' me at the same time, and Mr Peters is now standing next to us waiting in the rain, so I say bye to Hannah and her mum.)

Mr Peters: Oh, nothing very interesting. I went for some walks - there are some nice woodland areas near where I live. And I played board games with some friends, but I usually do that anyway. Then I was ill at the weekend so I spent Saturday and Sunday ill in bed. So, not very interesting.
(I say the board games sound fun and he says he's really into them. I ask him what his favourite is. He answers, but I've never heard of it. To be fair, he led with, "You won't have heard of it." He was right. I ask if it's a geeky game. He admits, yes, a bit, but states that there are far more geeky games in existence. I ask how nerdy his game is on a scale of one to ten and he won't settle on a number, maybe seven, but clarifies that Monopoly, for example,

isn't even on this scale. He takes pride in rising above Monopoly, and explains how really there's no skill in it, and something about probability, but he's half in his classroom doorway by now so we can't really get into the reasoning of it. He seems quite passionately against Monopoly, and I try to hide my amusement. I could have tried harder. I say now that he's dissected Monopoly, he's made it geeky enough to get on the scale.)

Note to self: I must talk less and listen more. I realise how much I tend to dominate conversation once I warm up, and it's annoying.

Tuesday:

What really annoys you?

Mr Peters: OK, there are two things. People who...
(He thinks. He wants to phrase it right.)
When your time is taken up unnecessarily. So... my job is busy, I've got lots to do, and if I have to spend a long time in training, learning something I already knew, like ten years ago, it's frustrating. And then, {the second thing that annoys me is} people who are in a role that's a position of power and they aren't in it for the right reasons.
(Pause. He looks frustrated at the thought of it.)
They see the title, but they don't see the real purpose of that role, they just want the power. As you can see, I'm not in teaching for the power!
(I say you have power over twenty five little people, half-kidding.)
Yes. But that's not why I do it.
(I feel this morning's is the most personal answer Mr Peters has given so far - he reveals the heart behind why he teaches. He looks at me intently and, between the lines, I understand that he is saying, "I could do other things that seem more impressive, but I choose to do this because I believe in it." As he speaks I can really see his authenticity in a way that he hasn't shown before. I feel like I understand him a bit better.)

Michaela: People who lie.
(She smiles, but it has sadness behind it. We both know why. I won't write it here. I say it feels like people who lie are a waste of time - how can you build any relationship with them without trust? We talk for a little bit about that and then about her tumble drier and hoover breaking, and how she is struggling with toilet training her new puppy.)

Steph: *(Steph isn't at at pre-school today.)*

Helen: *(Leo went home early today so I didn't see Helen!)*

Hannah: – *(I couldn't find Hannah in the morning and at the end of the school day she was hugging her Dad and looked upset, so I left her alone to give them some space. Poor thing. I hope she's okay.)*

Sidenote:
So far I've not had much luck this week; hopefully I'll manage to catch more people tomorrow. I have chatted with lots of other mums, too - other than Helen, Michaela and Steph - and I've been beginning to feel a bit less shy. Hooray!

Wednesday:

If you could master one new skill, what would it be?

Hannah: Backflips! And climbing up walls!
(She grins. "So basically you want to be Spiderman?" I say. "Yeah," she smiles. She seems really happy this morning.)

Mr Peters: *(He's very busy and a bit distracted this morning.)*
Time management?
(He laughs.)
Something more lucrative?
(He smiles.)
Sorry, I'm clearly in a sarcastic mood.
(Thinks…)
I started to learn to play the piano and read music, but got turned off it, and I'd like to have learned to sight read.
(I say you can still play piano without music. He says he knows but he just got really put off it. "You can't be good at everything," he grins.)

Michaela: *(Thinks…)*
Sewing.
("Hand-sewing or machine?" I ask.)
Machine sewing. Like my friend who's sewn a whole Pokemon costume for my daughter.
(I say I'm sure your friend would teach you but she laughs and says she doesn't have time.)

Steph: *(No Steph today.)*

Helen:

(Leo leaves at midday again today but I see Helen on her way out as I am collecting my youngest from pre-school. Helen's in her car with Leo but stops to chat; she says she's been missing our questions and thought of messaging them but realised that would defeat the object. I am so pleased, and point at her and say, "Yes! You get it!" I ask her today's question.)

To play the ukulele. Leo and I each have one and we strum away completely out of tune, and it'd be nice to actually play a real song.

Thursday: *(World Book Day)*

Where in the world would you most like to visit?

Mr Peters (Dressed as the Mad Hatter!): There's this place in Indonesia, it's like an orangutan sanctuary, and the orangutans have picked up human traits; there's one who saws wood, and one who washes socks. You can look it up on Youtube and see the video of it - it's under 'DIY Monkeys'.
(He's smiling throughout and seems thoroughly amused at the thought of it all.)

Hannah: *(No Hannah today!)*

Michaela: The Caribbean. Where it's hot!
(We get talking about Disneyland Paris, various holidays Michaela has had and fancy dress, as it's World Book Day today.)

Steph: *(Finally I catch Steph! We share our snow stories and I ask her today's question.)*
I want to say somewhere with sandy beaches, but maybe I should go for Portugal, because that's where my husband's family live. Hold on a minute, let me think about this... Sri Lanka ... I would say Australia but I'm not brave enough, with all the snakes and spiders. I'd love to go to Africa, but again I'm too much of a wimp. Where would you like to go?

(I say Iceland, and that I just feel a need to see the Northern Lights in my lifetime. Also New York. I agree with her about Africa, and say I'm so intrigued by it but the culture difference would obviously be a big challenge. Steph loves the idea of Iceland and NY and agrees she'd like to go to both. We get talking about the Scottish Highlands as neither of us have been beyond Edinburgh. It's a lovely chat and then the pre-school opens so we go inside.)

Helen: The Galapagos Islands. From a photography point of view, I've seen them so much on television programmes, and it just looks beautiful. How about you?

(The second time today that the question has been asked back to me - isn't that nice? I answer and Helen tells me that she's been to Finland and seen the Northern Lights and it's one of her Top 5 favourite places she's been. We talk about World Book Day and Leo's costume.)

Friday:

It's my birthday next week! How will you celebrate your next birthday?

Mr Peters: *(I say I watched the DIY Monkeys video and isn't it amazing? We discuss whether it's a bit sad that they mimic human behaviour with no understanding, but it's incredible nonetheless. Today is swimming morning so there are constant interruptions from parents and teachers asking him questions - he multitasks very well and we are amused by the broken conversation. Finally, he takes a breath and I ask Mr P about his birthday.)*
Well, my birthday was in January, and I don't really celebrate birthdays anymore, since I was about twenty-five.
(I ask if he did anything this year.)
I went out for dinner with my girlfriend, and… oh, the weekend before that I went for dinner with some friends and we went to the new Gin Bar in Exeter. So that's a lot more than I usually do.

Hannah: *(I couldn't see Hannah today.)*

Michaela: Nothing! My friends are all boring and I never have parties!
(She laughs. I ask when her birthday is and she tells me it's in July - it's after two of her kids' birthdays so doesn't really get celebrated. I say, "Next birthday - we're celebrating! I'll make you a cake." She grins and says, "Sounds good!" Pre-school is opening so she rushes in and we shout, "Bye!")

Steph: *(I didn't see Steph today.)*

Helen: By this age I just let them pass by and then you don't get any older!
(I ask if she has a takeaway or a cake and she says yeah, maybe a takeaway, but they hardly ever go out as it's so hard to get a sitter with Leo's medical needs. Helen says she's thought of a question for me… when was the last time you woke up naturally? Not from kids or an alarm? I say the last time was on the snow days, and that I lie in almost every Saturday morning, but I guess probably ultimately wake up from a sound of some kind. Helen describes this incredible recent nap that got her thinking about it, where she must have had the perfect amount of sleep because she woke completely naturally, and it was amazing. She asks what I'm up to this weekend and I say I'm having a little drinks party for my birthday, and we discuss drinking. I say I'm not really a big drinker. We have a giggle and it's a really nice interaction. I'd love to hang out with Helen outside of school some time; I really like her.)

Notes at the Weekend

What a lovely week it has been at school. It's hard to capture the precise feel of the conversations (though I have tried) but this week I feel like we all really got into the swing of chatting together.

I had a real laugh with Helen and am becoming such a big fan of hers. I love that she continues to ask me my opinions and preferences, too. She's not just wrapped up in her own world, but very thoughtful and otherly, perhaps sometimes to her detriment. I'd like to do something nice for her - maybe I'll bake her a little treat some time.

I keep struggling to catch Hannah - I think someone different was bringing her to school in the mornings which meant she was arriving a bit later. It meant that when I did catch her it was in the afternoons and it was brief - that was a shame. I loved that she wanted to be able to backflip - she enjoyed making me laugh with that answer!

I was delighted to feel my shyness break away with Mr Peters this week; our conversations felt much more friendly and familiar. We've now settled into a routine of chatting at the classroom door in the mornings, when I ask the daily question. He completely took me by surprise when he was dressed top-to-toe as the Mad

Hatter on World Book Day! I thought he didn't seem like the dressing up type, but how wrong I was! He was in his element! I feel like we clicked this week and we often had a laugh or shared a knowing look of amusement - I still find him a bit difficult to read but he's happy to clarify himself when I look confused (or when I ask him outright, "What do you mean?"). He doesn't seem particularly interested in anything about me but, then again, he is: a) not required to (!) and b) the only one who is at work while I'm grilling him.

And how different it is with Steph lately! I seek her out and we chat happily about whatever - I enjoy it. Even though I hardly caught her this week, when we did talk she was so warm towards me, I feel I've made a friend in her. She really does carry a sweetness with her, I hope you know what I mean, I'm not sure quite how to explain it better.

Getting to know Michaela is a more slow and steady process. I like her consistency - she can be refreshingly rational, but she's also always looking for a reason to laugh. I really like how into things she gets - down to the tiny details of her children's fancy-dress costumes, and the immaculate buffet she prepared for her son's baptism.

Aside from my five interviewees, this week I've had some nice moments at the school gates. I had a mum back to my house for coffee and that afternoon at school I saw she had headphones in and asked what she was listening to - she handed me an ear bud and we sat and listened together whilst waiting for our kids. I loved that! I have felt a change in myself and have felt relaxed enough to entertain other mums with funny stories and come out of my shell.

On a personal note, a few of my dear friends (not from school) have been having hard times for various reasons, and so this week has brought tears as well as the laughter and hard work which most weeks consist of. Life can be such a strange mix of joy and sorrow, can't it?

I'm having a bit of a party at my house tomorrow night to celebrate my birthday (I will be away on my actual birthday next week) and my little nephew is being dedicated at church on Sunday. I'm looking forward to a fun-filled weekend with friends and family.

Week 4

Monday:

What's something a tonne of people are into that you just don't get?

Michaela: Minecraft.
(She grins.)
I don't get it. I just don't get it at all.
(I ask her if her son plays it and she says he loves it. I say my answer would be eyebrows. She tells me she gets hers done once a month. She's running late so I say bye and let her catch up with her son at the nursery building.)

Steph: *(No Steph! Oh no!)*

Helen: I hope you don't find this offensive, but…
(I ask, "Are you going to say Disney?" - I ask because I write Disney-style songs which Helen has seen on Facebook.)
Yes! I just don't get it. And… I don't want to offend… are you religious?
(I say, "Yes. Well, I hate the word 'religious', but I'm a Christian.")
I just don't get religion. Well, I understand Christianity more, but I struggle with {some religions} and why they wouldn't let their child have a blood transfusion.
(She tells me about some people talking to her about God at her doorstep and when they saw her son with scars from his operations they recoiled. I say I believe God gave us intelligence and creativity to invent, and that operations are kind of miraculous in that way. I also say there are loads of weird or bad religious people and I totally understand her being put off. She asks what I think about evolution and how it's scientific fact. I share my annoyance at the

56

false God v. Science debate - I marvel at science and to me it's our discovery of what God has made. I explain how it's possible for evolution and the Bible to be perfectly in sync. Ultimately, I admit, if I didn't genuinely believe that God is real, I wouldn't see any point in religion. All I'm desperate to know is the truth. We are able to laugh and Helen says, "Well, that put the cat among the pigeons!" She says she hopes she hasn't offended me; I joke that I'm far more upset about her Disney answer! We laugh.)

Hannah: You-tubers. Like Dan TDM. Why does everyone like them? I don't get it.

(We all laugh. She tells me about a song/dance called 'Whip Whip Nay Nay' - apparently kids were dancing to it at the school disco. Hannah seems exasperated by the immaturity of her classmates, but can also see the funny side of her grown-up-ness.)

Mr Peters: Coffee. All hot drinks. It just doesn't make sense - why would you pour something hot into your mouth??

(He is smiling as he 'rants'. I clutch my chest and say, "It's like a dagger to my heart! And that's saying something because someone else's answer was God and religion!" He zones out slightly and remarks that he understands why people 'worship religion' - a phrase I find interesting, but leave - he pauses a moment, thinking, but chooses not to continue his train of thought. He comes back into focus and says he has never liked hot drinks. I observe that I've never known a woman who doesn't like hot drinks, but I know loads of men who don't. He mentions he has a female colleague who doesn't like hot drinks.)

Tuesday:

What personality trait do you value most?

Hannah: Being kind. And caring. When you trip over, they help you up, and when they trip over, you help them up. You know?
(I say I think it's because she is kind and so she's looking for that in others, and she agrees. Hannah's mum and I talk about their boiler; it has broken down.)

Mr Peters: Honesty. That's it - it's honesty. It's one of the reasons I became a teacher - because children either tell the truth, or they lie really badly and you can tell. I think that's changing, though, and I don't know whether they're getting better at lying or I'm getting worse at being able to tell.
(He laughs. He tells me that as a teenager and young adult he used to find it really frustrating when he couldn't tell if, or why, someone was lying. He tells me that he was speaking to his dad at the weekend about South Korea and his dad had told him that when he'd worked there, people would lie on a whim. It wasn't even with any purpose in mind, it was just a cultural thing. We continue to talk a bit about honesty but my younger daughter has run into Mr P's classroom and of course he needs to get on with the start of the school day so our conversation doesn't actually finish but we go our separate ways.)

Michaela: Loyalty. I think loyalty is the most important.
(Her answer is immediate and certain. She doesn't seem to feel the need to expand on this, which is quite usual for Michaela, and she moves onto another topic of conversation. We chat happily for a few more minutes.)

Steph: There are lots of good ones. Let me think. It's hard to choose. I think I'd say honesty. I think you can forgive someone most things if they are honest.

(I ask if honesty is an important value in her house, with the children, and she says it is. Steph says she's been thinking about the questions and that some of them are really good. She says the other day she was thinking about the "Where would you travel to?" question, and was thinking of loads of places and thinking she should make a list. She says she hadn't really thought about what she might like to do after the kids grow up. I think that is really interesting.)

Helen: *(Helen isn't here today - Roger is picking Leo up.)*

Wednesday:

What is your fondest childhood memory?

Hannah: *(Hannah's mum passes me on her way to her son's classroom and tells me that Hannah's not well today so she won't be at school. I tell her I'm going to be away for the rest of the week but will be back on Monday.)*

Mr Peters: *(Mr P is calming down a pupil who is upset so I say I'll catch him at the end of the day.)*

Michaela: Moving down to Devon to live with my sister.
(I ask where she moved from.)
Bradford. When I was fifteen.
(She tells me that her step-mum called her sister on the phone and said, "Michaela's moving out", even though it was the first Michaela had heard of it. She tells me that she came down on the coach on her own and I say it sounds like a sad memory but she says she was so happy to be coming to live with her older sister. Michaela says she was halfway through her GCSEs and the curriculum was different in Devon so she couldn't get into any schools and ended up learning in the community centre with pupils who had been excluded, covering material she'd learned back in Year 7. By the time she sat her exams, she says everyone else was finished and she was still writing; she needed more time. For a fond memory, this makes me feel so sad. Michaela is clearly an intelligent woman and it feels like she's got so much unrealised potential. She doesn't seem to feel this way, though.)

Steph: *(Steph grabs me in the pre-school cloakroom and says, "I want to change yesterday's answer! I've been thinking about it and what you asked about how I want my children to be, and it's kindness! It has to be kindness! Honesty is important too, but I want them to show kindness - even when someone is mean to them, because it might be the only kindness that person has been shown." Later, at pick-up, I ask about the childhood memory.)*

There are so many to choose from. I loved primary school. I loved holidays and Christmas. All of it, really. I need a day to think about these questions beforehand! It's really difficult to answer them straight away!

Helen: Probably going on holiday to Lulworth Cove in Dorset. Do you know it?

(I say I don't. Helen says that they moved about a lot so they didn't stay anywhere for too long. She asks me what my favourite memory is, and says she supposes I stayed put, but I say, "Actually, no, we moved about too." She says, "So you never had those forever friendships that have stayed through all of primary school?" and I gasp and answer, "Yes! Exactly!" I share how I've only recently realised that I form friendships very differently to others and perhaps it's because as a child I thought of friends as non-essential because we'd not be staying put forever. Helen says she envies people who have those lifelong friendships. She says it's hard now because she feels older than the other mums and wouldn't have anything in common with, say, a mum who is twenty-five. She also doesn't want to waste time with people she doesn't really get on with. I totally get it. We say goodbye and I say see you on Monday when I'll be a whole year wiser! We laugh.)

Mr Peters: *(He thinks.)*
My fondest memory... *(A parent approaches to talk to him and they have a short conversation. The parent leaves, and Mr P reclaims his spot beside me to answer the question.)*

I can't think of one fondest memory. Do you just want to know some things I enjoyed?

(I say yes.)

I enjoyed having a Lemming cake for my birthday with solid icing for the feet. I enjoyed discovering beach volleyball aged nine in India. I enjoyed going to Legoland in Denmark - that was pretty cool.

(He grins as he talks about his fun memories. I say bye and he walks the remaining children to their parents and calls back to me to have a nice birthday - very sweet.)

Thursday:

No Questions - Away at Conference

Friday:

No Questions - Away at Conference

Notes at the Weekend

Unfortunately due to the conference I was away at, we had to cut this week's questions short. I hope to make up the lost time with an extra week added on if my interviewees don't mind. Nevertheless, Monday-Wednesday was pretty interesting.

Monday's God-centred conversation with Helen was unexpected and I was thrilled to talk a little deeper, and about something key to each of our identities. Helen was so worried about offending me at the mention of religion that she sent me a message that evening checking I wasn't offended. (I got to use the laughing-out-loud Emoji for that one!) We both agreed that we're enjoying the questions and I made sure she knew how virtually impossible it is to offend me! I'm not threatened by anyone else's beliefs, because I have doubted and tested mine often enough. I am a deep thinker on a quest for the absolute truth, and I'm convinced of God's existence. I also understand why most other people aren't convinced.

Hannah was a happy little thing this week and I was glad I got to hang out with her and her mum a bit; I like them so much. We should hang out properly soon; we had their family round for a meal in the winter and I think another one is overdue! Hannah's description of what she looks for in a friend (that is how I worded the 'personality traits' question for her) was so simple and yet so wonderfully true. To pick one another up as and when we trip… children can have a way of summing things up so perfectly. They cut out all the frills and the rubbish and cut straight to the heart of the matter. It's one of my favourite things about kids.

I liked chatting with Mr Peters this week. I still always call him 'Mr Peters' - at first I felt like a ten-year-old calling him that, but now I've come to feel quite fond of it and think the name really rather suits him. It's a happy, friendly sort of a name.

It made me happy to hear Steph say she's been pondering on some of the previous questions - I think it's made a change for her to be thinking about herself and not always just the children. I thought that was quite cool! I think it's important to remember who we are and what we dream of.

I haven't felt a massive change or deepening in my friendship with Michaela but I do seek her out to stand and chat with, as she does with me. There's a simple but pleasing thing about that - it's like we're little girls at school, choosing each other for our P.E. team.

Week 5

Monday:

School closed due to SNOW!

Tuesday:

What makes you feel alive?

Mr Peters: Football. Five-a-side football. It's not that I'm really good at it, I just love it. When I was a kid I used to think heaven would be good if it was just a continuous five-a-side football game with all your friends on rotation and a supply of water.
(I say, "You used to think? Even now, that sounds pretty cool to me!" He says he realised there'd need to be more to it or it would get boring.)

Michaela: *(She thinks for a while.)*
Reading.
("You like escaping into another world?" I ask.)
Yes, exactly. Reading.

Steph: *(She 'ums and ahs' and tries to think.)*
When I was younger I would have said rides and things. Nowadays it's more like everyday things, really.
(I say that I asked my daughter and she said 'dancing', and for me it's making music. We talk about how wonderful it feels when the sun shines on your face.)

Helen: I know this might sound sickly-sweet, but showing people kindness. I get a real buzz from it. Like, I just helped this older couple to buy an iPad and now they are able to email and FaceTime their friends around the world. Also, being a mum, of course.

(We talk about World Down's Syndrome Day, which is tomorrow, and how we'll wear odd socks, but we'll have to be sure to wear shoes which will show the odd socks, unlike today, as we are both wearing winter boots. As I walk away, Helen suggests sandals and I call back, "Socks and sandals?? What are you thinking??" and Helen laughs.)

Hannah: *(I think Hannah is at home sick as I haven't seen her today.)*

Wednesday: *(World Down's Syndrome Day)*

What makes you cringe?

Hannah: When a teacher tells me off in front of the whole class. I'm like...
(She does an embarrassed face looking around. I say I wouldn't like that either. Hannah's mum says Aiden cringes whenever people kiss on TV, and she says TV marriage proposals make her cringe because they're so cheesy. She asks what makes me cringe and I say when people gossip - I feel so uncomfortable because I hate it and I just want the ground to swallow me up!)

Mr Peters: *(He compliments me on my odd socks, I say thanks and that they're my husband's.)*
Comedies like 'Meet the Parents' or 'Peep Show' where they set up awkward situations and you can just see it coming.
("So you don't like The Office?" I ask. He says no, and that he can't stand it. I say his answer surprises me because he doesn't seem to mind real-life awkward conversations; he says it's different because he can see it coming, and just goes ahead and has the conversation that's necessary. Whereas these movies and TV shows are contrived situations.)

Michaela: Chalk on a chalkboard, a knife on a plate, people grinding their teeth! I can't stand it! My son used to grind his teeth when he was little and it used to drive me nuts!
(We chat about Odd Sock Day and, along with some other mum-friends, show each other our odd socks. We agree it's good for our kids to understand more about Down's Syndrome.)

Steph: *(I'm a few minutes late for nursery pick-up and see Steph but not long enough to ask a question!)*

Helen:
(We chat for a full ten minutes about odd socks for World Down's Syndrome Day - about how supportive everyone has been and how crazy Helen's Twitter account has been going with responses and retweets of Leo's YouTube video for WDSD. We chat loads and then I realise I haven't even asked her a question yet, and I say clearly the questions work as we no longer need them to chat! I ask her the question anyway and she takes a moment to think.)
I can't really think of anything except when Leo used to click his hip in and out of place, that really made me cringe.
(We laugh and say, "Bye!")

Thursday: *(Sport Relief Day)*

What makes you smile?

Mr Peters: *(Mr P is wearing a football shirt with 'Stevie Wonder' printed across the back. He says it has a double meaning, it could mean he's a wonder on the pitch, or... I say, "You play football like a blind man?" and he says, "Exactly!" He can't stop grinning at his own joke. I ask what makes him smile and, ironically, he stops smiling in preparation for answering the question, which amuses me...)*
Satire? Can I just say satire? Satire, irony, clever tricks with words, all of that amuses me.
(His football shirt confirms his answer, eh?)

Hannah: When I see people. When I see my family.
(She is grinning from ear to ear.)
... and babies!

Michaela: My children. My children make me smile.
(She's grinning.)

Steph: *(I see Steph, and she says she's heard a rumour that chickenpox is going round the nursery class so is hurrying over to the school office to find out if it's true. If so, she says she will keep her youngest son out of nursery until the Easter holidays as they have a holiday booked and she doesn't want him to be ill and have to cancel. I ask the nursery teacher about it when I go in and she confirms that chickenpox is going around. This means I may not see Steph until after Easter! I haven't asked anyone about doing an extra week yet.)*

Helen: I smile to myself when I think of wicked practical jokes or pranks I could play.

(I laugh and ask if she ever acts on the ideas and Helen says, "Yes, sometimes… " I say, "Come on, Helen, you've got to give me an example!" She tells me a hilarious story about her partner over-worrying about her losing a fresh MOT certificate out of the window when Helen was driving in the car in front of him. He was winding her up driving too close to her car and trying to overtake, so she grabbed some blank loose papers and threw them out of the window as she was driving. Of course, he thought it was the MOT paperwork, stopped his car and chased after the papers all over the road! We laugh a lot. I say that I can't believe we only have one more week of questions, and would she mind if we did another week after the Easter holidays? Helen can't believe we're at the end of Week 5 and says, "Oh no! How about an extra two weeks, or four, or five?" I admit that I don't want it to end either and I'm getting addicted to asking questions!)

Friday:

What are your parents like?

Hannah: Nice. Kind. And loud!

(She chuckles. "Anything else?" I ask. She shakes her head, still grinning. She rushes into her classroom as she's running a bit late.)

Mr Peters: They're really boring. You're not printing my real name in this, are you?

(I say I don't have to if he doesn't want me to.)

Okay. Yeah, they're quite boring. Other people might find them interesting - they've led interesting lives.

(He lists examples of both of their incredible careers that are, actually, truly extraordinary. He says perhaps it's because his opinion of them was formed as a young teen when he was at boarding school, and he would just have a thirty minute conversation with them once a week. He says, "To give you an idea, my dad reminds me of John Major..." We laugh.)

Michaela: I never knew my mum, and my dad's an a***h***!

(I ask, "Do you want me to put that in print?" and she answers, "If you want!" I ask why she never knew her mum and she tells me that she died when Michaela was seven months old. I say I'm so sorry and she says it's okay and she dealt with it a long time ago. I ask if her big sister was like a mother to her and she says that she tried to be when Michaela moved in with her and it caused them to argue, and she moved out when she turned eighteen.)

Steph: *(No Steph.)*

Helen:
(First, Helen tells me some more of her wicked pranks, played mostly on Roger, and I laugh and gasp as she tells them. I tell her there's really no need for me to ask her questions anymore, let's just have a 'prank of the day', but she's keen to hear today's question, so I ask her about her parents.)

They're a bit rubbish, really. My mum wouldn't say she is an alcoholic, but she drinks throughout the day every day, and my dad is an alcoholic. They aren't together and so as children we were palmed off from one of them to another. They were just a bit rubbish. They are very kind people, though.

(She says she's made a deliberate choice to be a really good mum, very different to how her mum was, and we talk about how it's important to recognise generational habits or patterns, to decide whether to hold onto them or intentionally choose another way. Mr Peters pops outside to have a word with Helen about Leo so I try to remove myself casually from the now-three-person-conversation, overly aware of not wanting to intrude on their discussion.)

Notes at the Weekend

Firstly, what a weekend I had last weekend! I had an amazing birthday - songwriting all day in teams which actually, when I thought about it, was the best birthday activity I could have chosen! It was great. I loved turning a year older - introducing the new and improved, upgraded 'Jodie 32.0'! I intend to be more confident, relaxed, fun and open! And also to care less about what people think of me.

With this new positive outlook, I bounded through the school gates a new woman on Tuesday. I was in my element, chatting away to whoever might be interested. I enjoyed this week a lot.

I could feel that after the five-day break Mr Peters and I needed a few days to warm up again, which wasn't the case with the mums. Our chats are almost always cut short because of interruptions (he is, of course, at work, and so this is to be expected). I do genuinely find the various interjections amusing, but our conversations rarely have the chance to resolve of their own volition. I would love the chance to have a proper, uninterrupted chat with him; he is such good company.

It is now at the point with Helen, Michaela and Steph, where we are in the habit of chatting every day and I have to make a point of remembering that I'm supposed to be asking a question! I know for certain that after the six weeks are over, I will continue to have a laugh and chat with them every time I see them. Which kind of means that my idea works:

ask questions + listen to the answers = gain a friend!

I don't know if I will catch Steph at all next week as it looks like she will be avoiding pre-school like the plague! Such a pity! To make up for the snow days, and because term ends on Thursday rather than Friday, I'd love to do an extra week of questions after the Easter break. I asked Helen and she was very keen - I'm interested to see what the others think.

When I think about the questions coming to an end, my inner voice shouts, "Noooooooo!" I want to keep on asking and listening, it's lovely! I definitely think it's a great new skill to have learned and I've noticed myself asking questions all the time in all sort of different situations.

Yesterday after school, Michaela's son came back with us for tea and when I dropped him home, Michaela asked me in for cuppa and we chatted away for over an hour - it was great to have a more in-depth conversation. We agreed that Michaela and her three kids would come and play one day in the Easter holidays. Our kids play really nicely together.

Joff, the kids and I had brunch with our best buddies today. Tomorrow we've got church and a church-related teen pizza party at our house. So a pretty chilled weekend compared to last weekend. (We did two conferences back-to-back and it was incredible but intense!)

Week 6

Monday:

What's your dream?

Hannah: Bungee jumping! And I want to swim to France, and back!
(She's smiling but very sure of her answers!)

Michaela: To be a social worker. I've always thought I'd love to be a social worker. But I know I couldn't live with the decisions I'd have to make. I couldn't take children away from their parents wrongly, or have to walk away when I knew children weren't safe in their home. I couldn't do it.
(I can see a real passion for justice in Michaela, and a strong protective instinct for vulnerable children.)

Steph: *(No Steph.)*

Helen:
(Helen has had her hair cut at the weekend and looks amazing!)
Um…oh! To have a motorhome with beds and everything in it, and travel around and do home-schooling!
(Helen lights up as she talks about it, excitedly. Leo comes out of school and gives me a big hug!)

Mr Peters: What kind of dream do you mean?
(I reply, "Only you can answer that!" He smiles but looks puzzled.)

Do you mean like a Martin Luther King dream? Or a personal dream?

(I answer, "Your personal dream. Like, best-case-scenario for your life. Or something you just really want to do." He thinks for a minute or two, takes a breath and asks,)

Can I answer on another day?

(I say, "Yes." He says he needs to reflect on the question. He seems oddly thrown.)

Tuesday:

What's the best present you've ever been given?

Mr Peters: *(Mr Peters picks up right where we left off in yesterday's conversation. He takes a deep breath and leans against the classroom wall.)*

Okay. So I used to have a dream of having a house, and 2.4 children, and all of that. But something happened five years ago which meant that whole dream was dashed. And when you asked me that question, I realised, I haven't really thought about having a dream since then. I've never been the kind of person to have a clear, definite picture of what the future will look like.

(I ask if he would still like to have children. He says, "I don't think I can answer that. I don't just want children for the sake of it, it would be about that one person, who I was having the children with. And I suppose right now I can't picture the details of how that could work with my girlfriend and so it's hard to picture the future." I know from previous chats that his girlfriend lives several hours away so it's not particularly simple. He says he could give me a more throwaway answer if I'd like, and I say I don't want a throwaway answer; I tell him that I really appreciate his honesty, and thank him. We both feel the weight of the subject in a shared, sad moment. He warns there could still be a question that he just cannot answer, and I assure him I'm not planning to ask anything ultra-deep. I ask about doing a bonus week and he's fine with it. He changes his tone back to a more casual one as we head towards the next question.)

Okay, so what's today's question then?

(I ask. He thinks.)

OK, so I will give you a cop-out answer this time. For my 21st birthday, my housemates gave me a 1500-page

coffee table book called 'The Art of Looking Sideways'
and it was just a perfectly chosen book for me.

Michaela: My favourite present... a Mothers' Day
card that my son gave to me when he was two. He
picked me some flowers and made me a card.
*(I ask if she still has it and she says yes, she keeps everything and
her attic is full of all the things her kids have made. She says one
of the kids will draw a line on a piece of paper and someone will
go to throw it out and she says, "No, don't throw that away!" We
laugh. I admit I'm ruthless and only a small sample are kept -
Michaela is not impressed!)*

Steph: *(No Steph.)*

Helen: I don't know if it's the best one, but it's
certainly the most memorable. I had a blue velvet
pair of roller-skates in the 70s and I loved them so
much. I got them for Christmas and the reason it's
so memorable is that it snowed outside so I could
only use them inside and it was quite a challenge on
the carpet!
(We laugh, then chat about parents' evening, which is tonight.)

Hannah: My rollerblades. I got them for Christmas.
*(I ask what colour they are and she grins, "Purple." She tells me
she's going to her friend's house to rollerblade together later this
week.)*

Wednesday:

What's your favourite smell?

Hannah: Baby smell!
(I say, "Great answer! New babies smell so good, don't they?")

Mr Peters: Jojoba. I'm not sure how you say it. I think it's "Hohoba"?
(I admit I'm always unsure of how to pronounce it.)

Michaela: Baking. The smell of cakes baking.

Steph: *(No Steph.)*

Helen: Laundry. I'm obsessed with laundry smells.
(Helen tells me she has about seven different detergents and that she'll use different ones depending on her mood! She uses one scent for her sheets and Leo has his own scent! She just loves that clean laundry smell. This afternoon I've brought Helen some M&S chocolate eclairs - she hands one box back to me and says she really wants me to try them. We agree to both eat them tonight!)

I see Hannah and give her a box of Guylian to say thank you for all her answers - her face lights up and she looks so happy. I find Mr Peters and give him some oat cookies I made for him. I admit I wanted to make flapjack but have never really made it properly. He says it's really easy - I explain I didn't want to experiment on him.

Thursday: *(Last day of term)*

What music do you like?

Mr Peters: *(Mr Peters thanks me for yesterday's cookies and said he hadn't noticed the personalisation and thanks me for that - I had written a thank you note on the paper bag. It's the last day of term before the Easter break, and kids are handing him various chocolate treats as they arrive. He seems extra happy, as he always does at the end of the week and as all teachers do on the last day of term. My younger daughter stands with Mr P and me, talking to him about his chocolates, and making us laugh.)*
I can tell you some of the bands I like? I like strong female vocalists, like Paloma Faith. I like Pendulum... Aerosmith... Immortal Technique... The Go! Team (with an exclamation mark after the 'Go')... Glass Animals... Dire Straits... I like some classical music, like, is it Concerto in Em?
(I laugh and say it's funny he expects me to know - I really don't know my classical music.)
Who else is there? Garbage. I like Dan le sac and Scroobius Pip. I like Faithless. I don't like Ed Sheeran. I think that's probably enough!

Michaela: I like pop-punk. I like Avril Lavigne; her new album is brilliant.
(I say I didn't know she had a new album - Michaela gets out her phone and shows me it and a bunch of other albums on her playlist.)
I like Blink 182...
("I love Blink 182!" I chime in.)
I love Bowling for Soup, Lost Prophets, Nickelback, Daughtry. I like Ed Sheeran.

Hannah: *(I didn't catch Hannah today.)*

Steph: *(No Steph.)*

Helen:

(Helen has bought some Easter cupcakes from M&S for Saffy, my youngest child. She hands them to her and Saffy is very pleased!)

Lyrics are important to me. I love good lyrics. I really like Passenger. The lyrics are just incredible. I really like Counting Crows, too, but the lyrics just aren't there in the same way. It isn't always that clear what they're singing about, if you know what I mean.

(She says she'll message me some Passenger songs, as I tell her I haven't heard much of it. I say I really like Counting Crows, though.)

Notes at the Weekend

I am writing this on Thursday afternoon after school, having finished my questions for this term. Hannah, Helen, Michaela and Mr P have all agreed to another week of questions after the two week break, which I'm very pleased about. (I haven't seen Steph all week due to ChickenpoxGate but I know she'll be happy to do the extra week.)

Honestly, if I didn't know I had another week after Easter, I know I'd be feeling sad right now; I have enjoyed this experience so much beyond what I'd envisaged. I feel like my social muscles have been stretched and built up noticeably over this half term. I certainly feel bolder. But beyond that, I feel like I'm experiencing the beginning of real friendships and it's quite a special thing. I didn't want to say my goodbyes to everyone at the school run this afternoon. However, I will see Michaela in the holidays as I've invited her and the kids round to play!

It felt like Mr P. allowed himself to be better known to me this week. That felt like quite a privilege. I'll not see him for two weeks and will miss our daily chats. He works so hard all term, so it was lovely to see his big grin this afternoon in anticipation of a nice (well-earned) long break. I couldn't help but grin with him.

I missed chatting to Steph this week! I hope her little boy managed to avoid catching chickenpox!

Helen and I will no doubt keep in touch via phone messages - we've been sharing YouTube videos of songs we love!

I'm looking forward to time with friends and family over Easter - my friend Emma has told me about this cool co-operative board game she has called 'Pandemic' where you all work together to stop the spread of a disease around the world! So I'm hoping to have her over to play that with my friend Hayley and Joff and me. It'll also be Joff's birthday over Easter so that should be nice and will include some baking. We're having family to stay plus several friends with kids coming for daytime playdates. I'm hoping to let my other work calm down a bit and enjoy this time with the kids. Ooh, and we're heading up to Bath one day to see our friends James and Katy; we haven't seen them for ages! James is a composer and Katy is an actress - they kind of feel like our brother and sister. They are very dear to us.

I'll sign off here - see you in two and a half weeks' time for the final week!

Week 7

Monday:

What's your favourite season, and why?

Hannah: *(I couldn't find Hannah.)*

Michaela: Summer.
("That's no surprise, with your 'Caribbean' answer!" I say. She says, "Yep, summer, sun, I love it." She tells me she's found a nice route to my house from hers on foot - her and her kids took a teatime walk a few days ago.)

Mr Peters: *(We say hello and he thanks me again for the cookies and says they were nice. I ask today's question.)*
Summer. When it's hot... that's it.
(He smiles.)
I think you'll struggle to get any interesting answers to that one!
(I say "Well, some people might like Winter, being all cosy and warm inside.")
I grew up in India. It's got to be summer.

Steph: *(No Steph on Mondays.)*

Helen:

(I wait in the usual spot at the usual time, but Helen doesn't arrive. I pop her a message later to check she's ok; Leo had injured himself and been collected earlier.)

Tuesday:

Will you tell me something funny or embarrassing that's happened to you?

Mr Peters: Something funny or embarrassing... from any time in my life, or recently?
(I suggest that a recent story would be more entertaining. He really can't think of anything; he says he'll have to think about it and get back to me. He says he rarely feels embarrassed. I say I envy him that, and that I feel like lots of embarrassing things happen to me! "Maybe I'm just not much of a funny guy," he wonders aloud.)

I spot Steph at nursery drop off! We say, "Hi" and I find out that her youngest didn't contract chickenpox so they had their holiday! We talk about the Easter break and she seems very happy to do some more questions this week. We agree to catch each other at midday for a question at nursery pick-up time.

Michaela and I are having a picnic at 12.30pm so I'll ask her a question then.

Steph: *(Steph says she can't think of any, and says she'll need to think about it. Her youngest son runs off so she runs to catch him and we wave goodbye.)*

Michaela: The other night, the kids were in bed and I had a shower. I didn't have a towel in the bathroom so I walked across the landing (naked) thinking I was alone, and then I heard my younger son's voice... "Haha! Your bum is

enormous!" Then my older son started laughing too!

(We laugh a lot. I tell her about the numerous brutal truths or insults I've had from either my kids or kids at Sunday School. We have such a lovely afternoon at the park, watching our youngest children playing and chatting about everything and anything on the park bench.)

Helen: There are so many to choose from… I'll just give you a recent one. Leo and I were in the hospital. There was an older gentleman walking down the corridor who had clearly just had eye surgery and was wearing an eye patch over one eye. Leo jumped right in front of him and yelled, "Eye patch! Pirate's hat! Swashbuckle cheer - ya harr!"

(It's the theme song of a CBeebies programme. Apparently the man was mortified and Helen tried to explain about 'Swashbuckle' but in the meantime Leo had escaped into the gift shop and was causing havoc there.)

I get home later to find a message from Helen asking for an embarrassing story from me, and I am happy to oblige!

Hannah: *(I see Hannah on her way out of the gate with her dad. She seems flustered as I usually see her outside her classroom. She says she can't think of anything and takes up my offer of some more time to think!)*

Wednesday:

What one thing do you really want but can't afford?

Hannah: *(First, Hannah gives me her funny story - when she was little a dog ran into her and knocked her down to the floor. She giggles. I ask her what she really wants but can't afford.)*
A mansion.
(She grins, very happy with herself. I ask her brother what he'd like. He smiles and says, "A dog!")

Mr Peters: Okay, I've got a reasonably funny story. Believe it or not, I had to go on a Drivers' Ed. course a few years ago, and I was late for once *(he's usually an early person)*, probably from driving there carefully, and I asked someone, "Is this the Drivers' Ed. course?" and they said, "Yes..." but looked a little confused. Then when the teacher saw me, he kept doing double-takes and looking confused. It turned out I had turned up a week early, halfway through another Drivers' Ed. course...
(He says it was quite a few years ago now but he felt really embarrassed. He says usually he'd avoid embarrassing situations but it does take a lot to make him feel embarrassed. I tell him that on several occasions I've been washing my hands in a public bathroom, and have looked over to another sink and seen a man washing his hands, and we both have a look of confusion. Every time it's been a man in the ladies' loos. I ask what he'd really like but can't afford.)
Financial security.
(I pull a sympathetic face.)
Not that I'm not financially stable already - I have a good job and all that, and I'm lucky to have a job that I enjoy. But it would be amazing to have that complete financial

security - that you wouldn't have to do a certain job, or whatever. You could do what you really wanted. Those constraints wouldn't be there.
(I tell him he's talking to someone who has traded in financial security to do what they love. He doesn't seem to have any reaction.)
Yes, but it'd be nice to have both.

Michaela: To move to the Caribbean! Oh, or to go to Disney World in Florida! It would cost about ten grand to do it properly!! I'd love to go.
(I ask another mum who is a friend in common and standing with us, and we have a nice chat. I tell them about how I would love a Nord electric piano but it costs about £4000, and how I would love to buy it with money earned from songwriting or making music.)

Steph: I've been trying to think of something embarrassing, but I just don't feel embarrassed these days!
(We laugh. I say that's fine, and ask what she'd like but can't afford.)
A bigger house!
(She grins.)
In the countryside, backing onto fields.
(I ask if she'd like to have chickens and she gets all excited.)
I would *love* to have chickens. We're not allowed to where we live now. I don't know why, it was a weird rule when we bought the house - it stood out to me when I saw the word 'pigs' in there!

Helen: A motorhome. Either that or a trip to Orlando.

(I ask, "Why Orlando?")

Disney, of course!

(I look confused. "But you don't like Disney…")

I love Disney.

("Huh?" I am so confused.)

I was kidding when I said that before!

("Really? I seriously thought you meant it! I guess I didn't know you as well then?")

Exactly. If I said it now you'd recognise my sarcasm.

(We laugh. Helen tells me another embarrassing story which is mortifying and hilarious in equal measure!)

Thursday:

How do you wind down after a long day's work?

Mr Peters: Football. I realise that's been the answer to several questions. *(He laughs.)* **But I really feel the difference if I don't play.**
(He goes on to say that he plays on Tuesday and Thursday nights and he loves it. I admit I'm not into exercise but this time last year I was feeling some nerves/adrenaline about some upcoming 'unknowns', and I found that going for an evening run really helped. He says he agrees with one of Gandhi's philosophies that walking is good for you - to think, and not in a problem-solving way, but in a different, more spacious way. He says for this reason he will usually walk to football, to have some headspace.)

Michaela: A steaming hot shower, and reading a good book. Once the kids are in bed.
(She looks so relaxed and happy talking about it. I say, "Don't forget your towel, though!" We both laugh.)

Steph: A glass of wine, sitting on the sofa with my husband.
(Steph smiles. "Red or white?" I ask.)
Oh, red.
("I'm red, too," I say. I give Steph a thank you card and some posh crisps and thank her for answering all my questions. She says it's really got her thinking more and I admit the same. We say goodbye, knowing this was probably our last question.)

Helen: It's got to be a hot bath.

("Me too!" I chip in, and then I add, "I also do a face mask and it really relaxes me; I do it at least once a week." We gush over seriously hot baths and how relaxing and comforting they are, and Helen tells me that once she put a black peel-off face mask on in the day time, and then had a call from the school saying she needed to come in. The mask hadn't set yet and she was trying to quickly wipe it off, with much difficulty. We laugh as she acts out the scene!)

I've learned my lesson now - now I only ever do a mask at night time, once Leo is asleep!

Hannah: *(I didn't catch Hannah today.)*

Friday: *(The last question)*

How have you found this experience?

Mr Peters: I don't know if it's something you've picked up on, but I think I'm quite a reflective person - I'm pretty good at self-reflection compared to most people.
(I nod in agreement.)
But I've been surprised by areas I wasn't aware of, where it wasn't so easy to answer a question. I didn't really see that coming, and I found that aspect of it quite interesting.
(I talk about the social side of the school run from my point of view, and ask what he thinks about asking questions to get to know someone. He admits it's been very unusual getting to know each other this well as teacher and parent, and his challenge has been to maintain professionalism. I thank him, hand him a thank-you card, and make my way over to nursery with Saffy.)

Michaela: Intriguing. It's been intriguing, not knowing what the question will be each day, or how I will answer it.
(We both say we've enjoyed it. I ask if she thinks it's a good way of getting to know someone and she grins, "Definitely." I hand her a thank you card and we smile.)

Hannah: *(I find Hannah, give her a 'Minions' thank you card and thank her for everything. She's very smiley. I ask her how she's found the whole thing.)*
It was good! I really liked it! It felt like being on a game show!

(She says she doesn't want it to be over. She says maybe it's like a hidden-camera gameshow and we all laugh. I tell her I'll give her a copy of the book when it's done and she says, "Yay!")

Helen: It's been really interesting. I think if we hadn't had the reason to chat, we'd have just gone on nodding and waving for years, so it's been lovely to chat and laugh every day. On the days I haven't been here, I've been itching to know what the question is, and have really had to try hard to resist asking what the missed questions were!

(We agree how nice it will be to chat whenever we're both free and see each other at school. I hand Helen a thank-you card and she thanks me. Mr P comes out of school to go home for the weekend and offers us some sweets he's eating. I accept, as do each of my children; Helen says, "No thanks." Helen and I say we'll see each other tomorrow at the peaceful protest in our town against government funding cuts for schools.)

Final thoughts

It won't surprise you to read that I thoroughly enjoyed this final week. On Wednesday, the sun finally came out, marking the end of the season, and the start of a new one. Though a big part of me would love to continue, it did feel like the right time to finish the book.

Of course, this is not the end of a question-asking era for me, but just the beginning! I cannot write every conversation in this book, but since I have relaxed into the groove, friendships have been forming and - more importantly - deepening all throughout my life in different arenas. I've learned the power of listening, and the power of curiosity - taking an interest in the people I interact with each day.

I've realised, too, how very different people are, and find that fascinating! I also just think that at a fundamental level, as humans we long for real connection with others. It makes us come alive: encourages, comforts and inspires us. We are somehow truly nourished by eye contact, ears that are really listening, and a tap of the arm, a high-five or a hug.

I've also re-remembered what a gift I have in my
marriage - that I get to see my best friend every single
day. I get to laugh with him every day (truly!); share
curiosities or funny stories; and share heartbreaks,
disappointments and failures, too. I'm so, so lucky that
Joff and I are so alike in that we acknowledge our basic
need to connect and talk daily.

After seven weeks of questioning these five school gate
guinea pigs, I feel like I know them pretty well. With just
one daily, simple and usually light-hearted question, I
have become very fond of them all in different ways...

Hannah

Hannah is a sweetheart. She knows her mind! It's such a
lovely thing to see - a person who really knows who she
is, and what she likes and doesn't. She finds her security
and happiness in her family, and talks of them often.
Her parents are genuine friends to her, and she has a
very special bond with Aiden, her little brother.

She loves to learn and discuss new and interesting ideas.
Hannah is adventurous, extremely ambitious and
fearless! She is also extremely empathetic and kind-
hearted. She makes an excellent team-member and is
very pleasant and accommodating to work with. She has
a great sense of fun which is contagious to everyone
around her. She must never doubt her brilliance, and
know when to ignore undue criticism, and when to use

it to her advantage to help her become even more brilliant! My sense is that Hannah will be an unstoppable force of excellence and will achieve whatever she has her heart set on.

Helen

Helen has so many wonderful attributes, and I wish she truly knew how easy-to-like she is. She is warm, friendly, genuine, kind, and yet has this wicked sense of humour which sprouts from her brutal honesty, which I adore. She is: resilient, hilarious, optimistic and open-minded. I hope I can continue getting to know her beyond the pages of this book, because I think she is the kind of friend anyone would be lucky to have. She is independent out of necessity. Her challenge would be to choose to open up with others at a deeper level - to form a few of those strong, genuine friendships that provide support throughout all phases and seasons of life.

Helen is so dedicated to Leo, and their bond is something so very special. She knows she is lucky to have him, and he knows he is lucky to have her. It is beautiful to behold!

Mr Peters

I have found Mr P to be a highly intellectual, social being who finds comfort in his understanding of the world (and friends. And football!). I have a new favourite thing about him - I love the way he welcomes every single child by name each and every morning at school. He will make a wonderful father one day. Daily, and unprompted, Mr P reports positive behaviour or progress to parents in the presence of their children, and he is, in turn, very good at receiving praise and words of thanks (a sign of self-confidence, of which he has bucketfuls).

Mr P carries some rare and special attributes with him and doesn't seem to mind when no-one notices. He makes himself laugh a lot, and is very happy in his own company, especially in the great outdoors. He is not aloof, as I first supposed him to be. Darcie, Noah, Safferty and I (and even my husband, who knows him very little) are all very fond of him.

The adventurous experience of his childhood is a huge part of Mr P's identity, and if I could wish one thing for him it would be that he would step out and take some risks, and find some new adventures ahead. I sense there is so much more for him, in many areas of life! He has treasures inside of him that even he is yet to uncover.

Michaela

I feel like I am meeting Michaela at a really interesting time of her journey as a person. She is still so young (twenty-seven, if you remember!) and in many ways, didn't get to be a child for long. As she has shared her many stories with me (which are not included in this book), I've realised that I was so lucky to be born into the family I was born into. Michaela probably wouldn't say that about her family. And yet, here she is - this strong, beautiful woman, who has an inner sense of right and wrong, and a strong motherly instinct to protect others. She knows her value - that she deserves to be respected and loved.

I also love that she has not lost her voice! Life has not beaten her down - Michaela loves to laugh and is open about her pain, and able to cry when she needs to. She loves reading like no-one else I know. She loves trying out new recipes and plans the week's meals out with excitement and optimism. I know that her mother would be so, so proud of her, and of the mother she is to her three special children. I feel like Michaela is a goldmine of potential - I am so excited for her, to see what lies ahead in the coming years - anything could happen!

Steph

Steph is sweet through-and-through, and interacting
with her daily has made me realise that sweetness (the
genuine, pure kind) is actually pretty rare, and beautiful -
like a rare flower! Steph is like a refreshing aroma that
changes the atmosphere of a room - not
overwhelmingly, not even obviously, but it is a very real
change. She is kind down to her bones, and it radiates
from her, finding its home within and leaking out in the
words she speaks, the food she prepares, the smiles she
gives. But I hadn't noticed any of this before - writing
this all out has helped my brain to acknowledge what
my gut had already noticed. Isn't it strange? (Perhaps I
should keep a diary?) Do you know what is so cool
about her? Steph is a natural at being herself. I hope that
one day someone will say that about me. Don't you wish
that for yourself, too? I began by thinking Steph was
shy, but I think she is actually just an excellent listener
and happy not to be in the limelight, happy to do her
thing, without any need whatsoever for attention.
Through these questions, it has been lovely to see her
start to get excited about dreaming new dreams - I
wonder where they may lead her!

I hope you have enjoyed reading these conversations,
and that you appreciate how brave one initially-very-shy
woman has been to deliver them to you! But more than

anything, I hope to inspire you to step out of your comfort-zone and stop holding yourself back from the opportunities to grow deep and meaningful connections with those who live and work around you. It will look different with different people, of course. That's fine! You won't know why, but you will immediately 'click' with some people, and others may take time, but still turn out to be pure gold. Some may not be a fit or - truthfully - you may think someone is wonderful and want to be their friend, and they may not feel the same about you. (It's gutting, but learning to recognise it will save you some heartache! And eventually they might just realise how cool you really are.)

But take a few little risks and you will luck out eventually. Do you know why? Because you are surrounded by other people pretending to have it all together, who need friendship just as much as you do. I know it doesn't seem that way because we're a great bunch of actors, but I promise you, it's true. I have made you a list of easy-to-ask questions in the 'Questions you can ask' section to give you a kick-start! Promise me you'll give them a go at your school gates??

If you are wondering what will happen next for Hannah, Mr Peters, Michaela, Steph and Helen, then you are in good company! I will try to resist continuing to be so curious and grilling them daily. Hopefully we can just chat and all enjoy the pressure being off. I will still see all of them daily (except Mr P) for the next few years as we all have children in the same year groups. So I'm sure there is much fun ahead! But I do feel rather sad at the thought of leaving Mr P's classroom door at the end of the year - he has been such fun and refreshingly authentic company this year and I cannot reasonably expect to get on half as well with any other teacher - I realise it's extremely rare to get to know each other (and get on so well) as we have.

Finally, I'll direct my parting comments to my five subjects. Thank you to each of you for an eye-opening seven weeks! I really hope you enjoyed it, too, and please know that you all absolutely have permission to ask me questions to your hearts' content...

Questions you can ask

Questions are a great way to get a conversation started, with the pressure off you to talk - you're throwing the ball into the other person's court! And guess what I've learned? People are always happy to talk about themselves, and about their children! So stop thinking you have to be a stand-up comedian and just throw a question out there, and - most importantly - **listen to the answer.** Don't stress about what to say next. Focus more on listening. Otherwise the whole exercise is empty! The answer will either lead naturally to more questions or discussion, or you can leave it at that and chat another time.

Have you got any nice plans for the weekend/
Did you do anything nice at the weekend?

Do you know what the weather's supposed to be like this week/
weekend?

Is your child enjoying the class topic at the moment?

Is your child enjoying school? Did you enjoy school when you were
a kid?

Are you all ready for Christmas/Easter/Summer holidays?

Do you have any other children? How old are they?

Have you seen any good kids' films recently?

Are you into sports? Which team do you support?

Do you have any good tips for getting rid of head lice/getting your child to do their homework/getting your child to eat vegetables/ etc.? (People love to give advice!)

Have you done many birthday parties for {your child}? I'm thinking ahead for {my child's} birthday and trying to decide if a smaller or a larger party is best and if I should go for a venue or at home?

Have you read any good books lately?

Are you watching any good TV/Netflix series at the moment?

Do you know of any good play parks around here?

I'm a bit stuck in a rut for food ideas. What are your go-to weekday meals?

Does your child do any after-school clubs? Does he/she enjoy them?

Do you do yoga/running/evening classes? What do you do to relax in the evening?

Am I the only one drowning in laundry?? How many loads a day is normal?

Are you planning a holiday this year? What's been your favourite holiday so far?

Good luck - you can do it!